Three page foldout: Amish Church Service © 2000 Doyle Yoder. Forty-two buggies and the Church Wagon are parked at this home near Becks Mills in Holmes County, Ohio, on a crisp Fall Sunday morning.

An Amish couple head for Kalona, Iowa, early in the morning, perhaps to shop, deliver farm fresh produce or see a Doctor. The Amish use the horsedrawn buggy (or wagon) to run errands and visit their neighbors.
© 2000 Leslie A. Kelly

AMERICA'S
AMISH COUNTRY II

DOYLE YODER • LESLIE A. KELLY

A group of buggies head across a field to a cemetery in a heavy snowstorm near Farmerstown, Ohio.

No part of this book may be used or reproduced in any manner whatsoever without prior written permission except for brief quotations embodied in critical articles or reviews. Published by America's Amish Country Publications, P.O. Box 424, Berlin, OH 44610-0424 • First edition May 2000 Printed in United States of America • Library of Congress Catalog Card Number 00-190503 • **ISBN 1-930646-00-3**

FOREWORD

It has now been eight years since Doyle and I published **America's Amish Country** for the Tricentennial of the founding of the Amish as a religious sect. Much has happened in the past eight years for Doyle and myself and in the world in general. In America's Amish Country, however, little has changed for the Amish. They have new settlements in Maine, West Virginia and Washington. Their lifestyle continues at the same pace and in the same manner that it has over the past three hundred plus years.

America's Amish Country received many accolades for its photography and accurate portrayal of the Amish and their lifestyle. In response to the many requests for another look at America's Amish Country, Doyle and I have created another book that we hope will allow the *Englishers* to better understand the Amish lifestyle as portrayed through our images.

America's Amish Country II (*Revisiting America's Amish Country)* offers a fresh photo documentary of the Amish people and their unique lifestyle. It includes an overview of the Anabaptist movement as well as photography from areas in which the Amish lived in Switzerland and France. The expanded Lifestyle section depicts the Amish way of life that fosters close knit families, strong bonds with other members of their church district and the entire Amish community. Self reliance and work values are shown with threshing rings, field plowing, barn raisings, food preparation, pea shelling, vegetable garden work, young scholars, youth group activities, family picnics, fishing, sports, baseball, volleyball, horse shoe tossing and ice skating and other settings not shown in previous books. Special emphasis is given to children and their interaction with their parents that create such strong family bonds that few leave the Amish way of life.

Revisiting got its beginning in 1993 while I was making plans to attend the *Exposition Manifestations Publiques Coloque International à l'occasion du 300e anniversaire du mouvement amish 1693 - 1993* which was organized by the French Anabaptiste-Mennonite Historical Association. The event, held in August at Sainte-Marie-aux-Mines in France near an area where the Amish lived after leaving Switzerland, attracted hundreds of participants from Europe and the United States.

Doyle and I agreed on the need for a second book and that it should include photography from the scenic areas of Switzerland and France to illustrate the beauty of the areas from which the Amish originated. I found beautiful scenery and wonderful people in the Emmental area of Switzerland and the Alsace of France, both areas from which the Amish fled persecution before ultimately arriving in the United States. I understand clearly why they first settled in the hills of Lancaster County, Pennsylvania, and then created their largest settlement among the rolling hills of Holmes County, Ohio.

We believe that **America's Amish Country II** continues the accurate portrayal of the Amish and their lifestyle in the tradition established first by **America's Amish Country.** We hope that you agree.

I wish to give special thanks to my wife Cathy, a wonderful travel companion, and a special wish that our grandchildren Christopher, Lucas, Cameron and James have the opportunity to travel and see the beauty and diversity of the world as we have been able to do.

Leslie A. Kelly

Leslie A. Kelly

I wish to thank all my Amish neighbors and friends here in Holmes County and friends in other communites across America who have tolerated and been cooperative to me and my camera. But most of all, and most important, my thanks go to God for his wonderful creation, the splendor of the seasons, the formation of the mountains, the rolling hills and the prairies from the master painter who gives me the opportunity to capture it on film and share with others.

Doyle Yoder

Doyle Yoder

My favorite photography subjects come together, Amish country and Trains near Nappanee, Indiana   D.Y.

Our Cover Photo

About the cover of **America's Amish Country II.** If you think that it looks just like **America's Amish Country,** you are correct. It is the same farm in Holmes County painted in fall colors.

As a young boy growing up about one mile from this farm near New Bedford, Ohio, I rode my bicycle past here many times. I always came up this hill, stopping for a while to rest and

enjoy the views. Looking north towards Charm and Farmerstown, you could see over a dozen farms, but this view facing south with its winding country road is still one of my favorite. This is a typical Amish farm with the main house, *dawdyhaus* for the grandparents, big barn with straw shed attached, pasture in the bottom land and crops planted in rows on the hillsides. As you can see, the farm looks beautiful in all sea-

sons and the scenes from the other side of this farm are just as good!

Does this mean that there will be more editions of **America's Amish Country**? Time will tell, of course, as there are two more seasons for the cover and lots more pictures in our files that have yet to be published. And, in a few more years, there will be even more.

Doyle Yoder

3

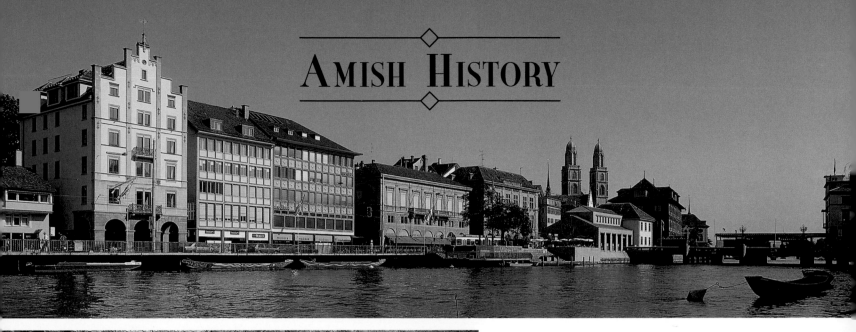

AMISH HISTORY

Above: The Limmat River, scene of many drownings of Anabaptists, flows through Zurich, Switzerland. The twin towers in the background are from the Grossmünster, a Protestant church founded by Charlemagne in the 800s AD. *Left, above:* The Täuferhöhle, "cave of the Anabaptists," was a secluded cave used by the Anabaptists for secret church services near the very small village of Wappenswil. *Left, lower:* This barn, on the Fankhauser Farm near Signau, houses the last known hiding room for the Anabaptists. *Bottom left and right:* The hidden hole in the floor had black covers to pull over to help conceal anyone who might be hiding below.

The Amish trace their origins to the Anabaptist movement of 1525 in Zurich, Switzerland, at the time of the Reformation. Anabaptists preferred to remain apart from other groups that might try to change their ways and baptized adults, which the Catholics and Protestants considered heresy, rather than infants, as the State had mandated. They held church services in their homes to avoid persecution by state and church authorities. Despite the death of many Anabaptists at the hands of zealous conformists, often drowned in the Limmat

River in Zurich as heretics, the movement survived as the Anabaptists scattered into the Emmental area near Bern. From then until the early 1700s, many were forced from their homes and fled to Holland and the Palatinate (Germany).

In 1563, a Catholic priest named Menno Simmons joined the Anabaptists and then formed a separate group known as the Swiss Mennonites. Forty years later, in 1693, during a minister's meeting of the Swiss Mennonites at a farm near Fridersmatt, Jacob Amman, one of its bishops, broke away from that group when it refused to enforce the *Meidung*, the shunning of excommunicated members. Others joined with Amman and became known as the Amish Mennonites. By 1696, they had moved to near Ste-Marie-aux-Mines in the Alsace Region of France. In time they became known as *the* Amish.

During the early 1700s, the few remaining Amish families located in the Emmental and the Lake Thun area (near Bern) either moved to

France or was assimilated into the Swiss Mennonites. Because of continued persecutions from 1710 until 1730, many moved into southern Germany, Luxembourg and other areas of France. From the late 1720s, the Amish took advantage of the opportunity for religious freedom as part of William Penn's "Holy Experiment" in his Pennsylvania Colony. The first documented arrivals sailed from Rotterdam, Holland, and

Above: This field in the Emmental was cut by scythe and the bundles tied by hand and left to dry. *Below:* Beautiful flowers and wonderful scenic views from this farmhouse is typical of many of the centuries old country houses in the Emmental.

arrived in Philadelphia on October 2, 1727. Migrations continued until the mid 1800s when all of the Amish had either moved to the United States or

had been assimilated into the surrounding Mennonite and Hutterite communities in Switzerland, Germany, Holland, France and Russia.

In Pennsylvania, the first Amish immigrants to America in the early 1720s settled in Berks, Chester and Lancaster Counties. Indian raids in Berks County in the 1760s caused those early Amish settlers to move, settling in Mifflin or Somerset

County, Pennsylvania. New emigrants and Lancaster area Amish seeking more land settled in Somerset, Mifflin and Union Counties in the mid- and late-1700s. Holmes County, Ohio, was first settled in 1808.

The Amish have expanded their settlements into twenty-four states (Ohio, Pennsylvania, Indiana, New York, Maine, Delaware, Maryland, Virginia, West Virginia, North Carolina, Florida, Texas, Tennessee,

Above: Jacob Amman was born at Erlenbach, seen here in the distance on the mountainside, in the Simmental Region. *Below:* Amman stayed in this house near Fridersmatt when the schism between the Swiss Mennonites and the Amish occurred. The meeting of the Swiss Mennonite Bishops took place on the nearby farm of Bishop Milaus Moser in July 1693.

Kentucky, Wisconsin, Minnesota, Michigan, Illinois, Iowa, Missouri, Kansas, Oklahoma, Montana and Washington) and the Province of Ontario, Canada. The Amish population is estimated at least 150,000 counting only adult churh members. The Amish of Lancaster, Pennsylvania, are perhaps the best known because of the many tourists who visit the area and the movie, *Witness,* which was filmed there. Holmes County, however, is home to the largest Amish settlement in the world.

Today the Amish live their chosen lifestyle and practice their religious beliefs in freedom without fear of persecution.

6

Above: Jacob Amman moved to this beautiful valley near Salm, Alsace, France, in 1693 soon after the schism between the Swiss Mennonites and the Amish. Some one hundred Amish families lived here until they departed for America in the 1720s. *Below:* The Jonas Stutzman farm as it appears today, the oldest Amish homestead in Holmes County. *Center:* This picture of the Stutzman farm was taken sometime between 1860 and 1880. The Amish began moving into Holmes County, Ohio, in 1808.

THE AMISH LIFESTYLE

The horse-drawn buggy is the best-known symbol of the Amish to the curious *Englisher,* Yankee or High People (names given by the Amish for anyone who is not Amish) who stare at them from passing cars and tour buses. Known as the plain people because they wear plain colored clothing, they live in farmland locations across America. The Amish — who speak Pennsylvania Dutch among themselves — live within highly personalized relationships, avoiding more than casual contact with strangers who might attempt to educate them to the ways of the outside world. Even though the Amish avoid most of the conveniences of the Twenty-First Century, something that most outsiders have difficulty understanding, they are happy in their way of life.

The history of the Amish is a mirror of their lifestyle and their religious beliefs. Born into existence at the height of persecution by Catholics and Protestants alike, the Amish and their lifestyle are an extension of that Reformation era struggle. The *Ausbund,* the Swiss Brethren hymnbook originating from the late 1500s, is still used by the Amish during their church services. It is considered the oldest hymnbook in continuous use by a Christian group. Anabaptists wrote many of its hymns while they were imprisoned in dungeons for their religious beliefs. Even today the Amish reflect during their church services on the struggles of their Anabaptist and Amish Mennonite forefathers in Switzerland and Germany more than four hundred years ago. The Amish hold their church services in the homes or barns of their members, a practice carried over from Europe when they did so in secret to avoid persecution for their religious beliefs.

Several obvious symbols of their lifestyle resulted from persecution at the hands of government soldiers, dressed in fancy uniforms with large buttons and sporting mustaches. The pacifist Amish do not use buttons and the men do not grow mustaches to avoid any resemblance to the military.

The Amish remember the past and pray that they will not have to endure the persecution for their desire to live apart from the world around them. They don't condemn the practices of the modern world; they just don't want to be a part of it. This lifestyle decision is based upon Romans 12:2: "Be not conformed to this world, but be transformed by the renewing of your mind that ye may prove what is that good and acceptable and perfect will of God."

There is no so-called "Amish religion". The Amish are Anabaptist and follow the teachings of the Bible and Jesus Christ. The term Amish comes from their founder Jacob Amman. The foundation for their faith is the Bible that they interpret literally; the *Ordnung* is the basis for their lifestyle. The local church district Bishop sets "Rules of order," or the *Ordnung,* that cover every aspect of their lives. They include types of buggy wheels, length of hair for men (the women do not cut their hair), width of hat brims, etc. The "Rules of order," with slight differences, explain the variances found between Amish communities. These unwritten rules are memorized from youth by the members and govern the church district's daily life.

Some groups, based on the local *Ordnung,* allow a more tolerant lifestyle than others. The clothing rules in Indiana are not as strict as those of Holmes County, Ohio. Amish men wear beards based on a biblical passage that states that they should not mar the hair on their face (Leviticus 19:26). Young men are encouraged to grow beards as early as possible but must do so, unless they are physically incapable, upon marriage. Old Order wear their beards longer while

This box, resting on a church bench, is used by an Ohio Amish church district to store copies of the *Ausbund* and other church related books. The open books are, from left to right, a condensed version of the *Ausbund,* the full version of the *Ausbund* and the German New Testament. In the top of the box, the large books are the full version of the *Ausbund* and on the right is a small Prayer Book. These books along with the church benches are kept in the church district's "church wagon" which is moved from house to house where church services are held. The family hosting the district's church services will clean their house thoroughly, sprucing up the interior and exterior to show it at its best! In cold weather furniture is moved out of the main rooms of the house to make room for the church benches. In warm weather church services are held in the barn, buggy shed, shop or other out buildings. After the church service, the benches and books are returned to the "church wagon" and it is moved to the home of the next family to host services.

the New Order keep them neatly trimmed.

The more conservative groups, such as the Swartzentrubers and related groups, and some Nebraska Amish of Central Pennsylvania, avoid indoor plumbing, do not use motorized horse drawn equipment of any kind and wear conservative clothing. The Nebraska Amish do not wear suspenders or bonnets and are not permitted to have screens on their doors and windows.

Deeply devoted to their religious beliefs, the Amish hold church services every other Sunday. Songs from the *Ausbund* are sung slowly, *a cappella*, as the Amish do not play musical instruments. The sermon is conducted in German. The approximately three-hour service is followed by lunch and several hours of socializing. Services are rotated from house to house in their church district. Many of the Amish will travel to services at another nearby church district when their district is not holding services.

By having each family in the church district host services, the task in preparing for the service and preparation of food is shared evenly. This also allows the Amish to monitor the lifestyle of each family to assure compliance with the rules of the church. Those who do not are confronted. If they refuse to comply, they are shunned (*Meidung*) until they either comply or are excommunicated from the church. Amish youth usually join the church in their early twenties. They can do so earlier but must do so before they marry. They are not forced to join; however, most usually do because of their strong faith in the Amish lifestyle.

A church district usually consists of twenty-five to thirty families in a settlement. When a settlement grows larger, additional church districts will be created. Often times, members of different church districts will join with their Amish neighbors to help each other with threshing, field plowing and barn raisings as well join in quilting circles. These rings, as they are often called, take on the tasks made easier by many hands in support of their neighbors. In times of disaster or major need, Amish neighbors pitch in to help their *Englisher* neighbors as well.

The Amish people do not pose for pictures because they believe that photographs violate the biblical teaching against making graven images based on Exodus 20: 4: "Thou shalt not make unto thee any graven images, or any likeness of any thing that is in heaven above, or that is in the earth beneath, or that is in the water under the earth." Also, they are concerned that pictures of themselves will promote self-pride. They may put their hand or hats over their faces, look away or take evasive action to avoid having their picture taken.

AGRICULTURE IS THE PRIMARY LIFESTYLE

The Amish are primarily farmers since this allows them to be self-sustaining and live apart from the world around them. Some, however, are carpenters and cabinet makers, blacksmiths, buggy and harness makers, all geared toward supporting the Amish lifestyle. Because farmland is expensive, and becoming increasingly scarce, some younger members have taken jobs in nearby factories and restaurants. Others work in general stores that provide the Amish community with goods necessary to their lifestyle that they cannot produce themselves. The Amish lifestyle is very much like that of the *Englisher's* ancestors of a century or so ago.

Their neat Amish farms, without electric and telephone lines, look much like those of the *Englishers* around them. The houses are comfortable structures with numerous rooms to support typically large families. Many of their conveniences were used in America's Nineteenth Century or earlier houses. Wood or coal fueled stoves provide heat. Cooking stoves are powered by wood, propane, natural gas, or kerosene. Kerosene or clear gas lamps provide light.

A distinctive feature of America's Amish country is the windmill, used to pump water for house or farm use. While some also use gasoline engines to operate pumps with pressure tanks to provide running water for bathrooms and kitchen sinks, the old-fashioned hand pump is still used in many houses.

Some use kerosene-fired water heaters. Others run a system of pipes through the kitchen stove (fired with wood, kerosene or propane) to obtain hot water for kitchen or bathroom use. Those lucky enough to have natural gas on their property will use it to heat their house, provide hot water, fuel their refrigerator and provide light at night. Colorful flowers brighten the ever-present "kitchen gardens". Quilts decorate bedrooms while calendars with scenic pictures, meeting the requirement of utility, cover many of the walls of their houses.

LIFESTYLE SEEMINGLY PARADOXICAL

A number of paradoxes seemingly exist as the Amish strive to maintain their simple lifestyle in the Twenty-first Century. While horses pull things with wheels, some groups use gasoline engines to power agricultural implements and other equipment. Air tires are replaced with steel or solid rubber and the drive shaft, designed for connection to a tractor, is fitted to a small engine with a pulley and belt. With the increasing influx of tourists to their areas, many take the opportunity to sell excess farm produce in season as well as some baked and canned goods to raise cash.

Although Amish people cannot own or drive vehicles, they do travel by train or bus and ride in cars and trucks driven by others to visit friends and relatives or to take vacation trips to scenic areas. Neither electrical appliances nor telephones are found in Amish houses (although a few New Order churches now allow electricity and telephones). They will use (public or English neighbors) telephones to make doctor appointments, hire drivers (of vans) to take them for a doctor's appointment at a distance or to visit friends and relatives beyond a buggies' range.

AN ENDURING LIFESTYLE

While the Amish lifestyle to an outsider may seem austere and out of sync with the world around it, the Amish way of life fosters close-knit families, strong bonds with other members of their church district and the entire Amish community. The Amish consider self-reliance and work values a virtue, something that is admired by those *Englishers* who observe them from their cars and buses.

There are now more than 150,000 adult church members in twenty-four states and Ontario, Canada. Despite the few who leave the faith each year, their population has been gaining in total number. This is due chiefly to increased longevity common to the general American population and families that average seven children.

While most immigrants are assimilated into America's culture, the Amish remain a religious community forming a subculture more than three hundred years after their arrival. Although the Amish are seemingly a paradox in Twenty-first Century America, they live a lifestyle that allows them to comfortably and peacefully follow their religious beliefs.

THE AMISH FAMILY

The Amish lifestyle is built around highly personalized relationships between the biological family and their extended church families. Amish families within settlements visit each other frequently. Socializing among family, friends and neighbors is extremely important to the Amish. They may visit with a local family member or neighbor after chores are completed, or at an auction or "frolic" during the day. Distant friends and relatives remain in contact by mail and, in cases of emergency, by telephone.

When the older family members "retire" from farming, they move into a "Grandpa House" or *dawdy haus* adjacent to the main farmhouse. They continue to work, performing useful chores around the farm, while retaining a strong sense of independence. They are also snowbirds. There is a retreat for the elderly members in the Pinecraft area of Sarasota, Florida, where some go, usually during the winter. The Amish see no problem with this since most of those who visit Pinecraft are the older, retired people who maintain the same lifestyle as back home. Besides, it allows them the opportunity to visit with others — one of the basic pleasures enjoyed by the Amish.

Amish people will not accept public welfare aid or retirement income. They do pay income and real estate taxes just like the *Englishers,* but are exempt from social security taxes if they farm or are self-employed.

Amish parents treat their children with deep respect and love. The children help with chores around the house and farm as soon as they are able to do so. Children are involved in all activities with their parents. They will accompany them on errands, work, church and social events. The Amish are not distracted by modern inventions that separate family members from each other, such as "day care," radio and television, the computer and other forms of entertainment popular with the outside world. The closeness of family members helps create a bond that endures throughout their lifetime.

Until they start school at the age of six, most Amish children speak "Pennsylvania Dutch," a German dialect. Most attend parochial schools where they study English and German along with the traditional subjects of reading, writing and

Amish horse-drawn buggies, with children looking out the back, are a common sight on the roads around Allensville, Pennsylvania, and throughout America's Amish Country. This family buggy will seat up to eight adults and children comfortably. Occupants are kept warm in the winter with wool blankets. Some buggies may also be equipped with small clear gas or propane heaters. *Above:* This Amish father carries the diaper bag and a lantern at Topeka, Indiana, while the mother cuddles their infant child, as they walk to a family gathering that will extend past sundown.

Above, left: A father adjusts the suspenders of his young sons to assure a good fit at the machinery sale in Kidron, Ohio. *Above, center:* During a quiet moment, a father sits with his children seen here at Holmesville, Ohio. *Above, right:* A young couple pulls a wagon with their three small children while on the way home from church services in Spring Garden, Lancaster County, Pennsylvania. *Center, left:* Amish children enjoy wading and splashing in a small creek at a park in Middlebury, Indiana. *Center, middle:* Three generations of a family shop at the Topeka auction in Indiana. Grandparents often help their children with errands. *Below, left:* The children in the back of this open hack (wagon used to haul things) are amused by the dog running alongside them at Rebersberg, Pennsylvania. *Below, right:* Father and son enjoy a treat of ice cream while attending the auction sale at Belleville, Pennsylvania. They are members of the Nebraska Amish, also called the "Brown Amish," one of the strictest groups within the Old Order.

arithmetic. However, in those counties predominantly inhabited by Mennonites, many Amish children may attend public schools. Whether attending public or private schools, they only attend through the eighth grade.

The New Order church districts have taken steps to counter the Old World custom of bedroom courtship and allowing the young to "sow their wild oats" before marriage and their entry into the church. In an effort to provide alternative social activities, similar to programs designed to keep *Englisher* youth off the streets, church ministers meet with the youth to sing hymns and talk.

A few Amish youth and even adults leave the Amish lifestyle. They often affiliate themselves with a local Mennonite church. The majority remains because of their strong religious beliefs and the enduring relationships that the Amish families enjoy within their highly personalized world.

CHILDREN

Children have the opportunity to go with their parents on errands as well as the opportunity to have fun when their chores are complete. Older children often take care of younger brothers and sisters so that their parents can tend to fieldwork or housework that would otherwise be too distracting or dangerous for the little ones to be near.

Above, left: A young boy offers a friendly smile at the Kidron, Ohio Auction. *Above, right:* Older girls sit with their younger siblings while they wait for their parents at the sale barn at Middlefield, Ohio. *Center:* Girls give a friendly wave in Brush Valley at Rebersberg, Pennsylvania. *Below, left:* Three girls enjoy playing in a creek at Middlebury, Indiana. *Below, right:* An older girl plays with her younger brothers and sister near Holmesville, Ohio.

Above, left: Two girls sit at a social gathering near Topeka, Indiana. *Above, right:* Two girls enjoy a laugh while attending a barn raising near Holmesville, Ohio. *Center, left:* Youngsters play in a Lancaster County "gray top" buggy at Quarryville, Pennsylvania, in Lancaster County. *Center, right:* An older Amish boy holds his little brother with a "teddy bear" at Middlefield, Ohio. *Lower, left:* A young girl pulls her even younger sisters in a small cart at Mt. Hope, Ohio. *Lower, right:* Two young boys play in a home made wagon near Walnut Creek, Ohio.

13

Above: Children head to the schoolhouse across a large schoolyard near Maysville, Ohio. *Below:* Barefoot, with lunch pails in hand, these two scholars have walked through fog to get to their schoolhouse near Kidron, Ohio.

SCHOOLING

Scholars, as Amish students are called, attend school at a nearby Amish schoolhouse throughout much of America's Amish Country. They attend from the first through the eighth grade where they study reading, writing and arithmetic. While the Amish have enjoyed freedom to practice their religion of choice in the United States, their lifestyle was challenged in the 1970s over schooling of their children when three Amish fathers were arrested in Wisconsin for failure to send their children to school until age sixteen. They believe that formal training beyond the eighth grade does not increase their knowledge and skills as much as that which they learn from their parents and neighbors to become farmers and homemakers and to pursue their chosen lifestyle.

Interested church groups mounted a legal challenge on behalf of the Amish and won their case in decisions that ranged from a local court in Wisconsin to the United States Supreme Court. In 1972, in the case of Wisconsin vs. Yoder, the court ruled that it was unconstitutional to force the Amish to send their children to high school. Chief Justice Burger wrote: "It is neither fair nor correct to suggest that the Amish are opposed to education beyond the eighth grade level. What this record shows is that they are opposed to conventional formal education of the type provided by a certified high school because it comes at a child's crucial adolescent period of religious development."

14

Above: This schoolhouse, outside Milverton, Ontario, is set up for children to return to class in September. *Below, left:* Decorated paper plates indicate the birthdays of the school's students. *Center, right:* The school bell stands ready to ring in the students from the schoolyard. *Lower, right:* Paper and ruler await the return of the scholars from summer vacation.

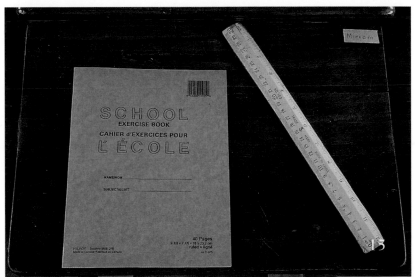

Above: Parents prepare to paint this schoolhouse near Intercourse, Pennsylvania, while young children watch carefully. *Center:* Scholars enjoy a spirited game of baseball at this schoolhouse near LaGrange, Indiana. *Lower, left and right:* Students leave the schoolhouse for the walk near Rockville, Indiana.

Above, left: Children arrive at school on a beautiful fall morning near Middlefield, Ohio. *Above, right:* Two boys, pulling sleds, and a girl walk in a heavy snowstorm to get to their school, in the distance, near New Bedford, Ohio. *Center:* Heavy snows make for great sledding out back of the schoolhouse.

Lower: Ice-skating on a pond near Dalton, Ohio, is great fun.

All children love horses and animals and the Amish are no exception. Ponies, carts and children just seem to be a natural. Their play teaches them practical lessons for when they are older and ready to take a buggy on the road or work with a team for plowing in the fields. These scenes are from *(Above)* Goshen and *(Inset)* Middlebury, Indiana; *(Below, left)* Farmerstown and *(Lower, right)* Charm, Ohio.

Above, left: This young boy rides a mule at Jamesport, Missouri. *Above, right:* Amish children may adopt wild animals as pets such as this baby raccoon at play on a shock in a field near Charm, Ohio. *Center:* Cats enjoy a fresh pan of "udder" warm milk in this barn near Charm, Ohio.

Below, left: A young boy herds the cows to pasture through this authentic covered bridge constructed by its Amish owner near Charm, Ohio. *Below, right:* With milking complete, these boys finish their chores by walking the cows back out to pasture near Berlin, Ohio.

19

Page 20. *Above, Left:* A young boy wheels a large block of ice into the house at Farmerstown, Ohio. While some Amish use natural gas or propane gas powered refrigerators, many still use ice to keep food cold. *Below:* An older boy hitches up with a pony to plow the small kitchen garden at this home at Bunker Hill, Ohio, while his little brothers and sisters watch.

Above: This young boy handles a team of horses and manure spreader to fertilize this field in Fairbank, Iowa. Although he is only thirteen years old, he has already learned many of the skills necessary to become a successful farmer. *Below:* Although these children are too young to actually work in the fields, they enjoy the ride home from the field and gain knowledge from the experience with a hay cutter (*Left*) near Mt. Hope, a hay wagon (*Center*) near Charm and a disc (*Lower*) near Bunker Hill, all in Ohio.

21

YOUTH

Amish youth socialize in groups whenever possible at an evening youth gathering after chores are finished, Sunday afternoon gatherings after church and for the traditional Sunday evening hymn singings. Relationships that lead to marriage usually are formed during these activities. Open dating does not take place but the boy and girl have time to talk after church services, at barn raisings and frolics, picnics and youth activities such as volleyball and baseball. While a girl will not ride with a boy to a Sunday evening singing, she will ride home with him afterwards in the dark. The boy will visit at her house only at night after the parents have gone to bed. This courtship, usually conducted in secret, has become more open with New Order Amish in recent years.

Page 22. *Above:* A group of young girls at play after helping maintain this beautiful garden near Topeka, Indiana. *Below:* These Nebraska Amish girls are lined up along the fence to watch a barn raising near Milroy in the Big Valley, Pennsylvania.

Above, right: A young girl looks pensively out the window of her house at Farmerstown, Ohio. *Center, left:* A group of boys walk down the road on a Sunday afternoon near Quarryville, Pennsylvania, on their way to an evening gathering. *Center, right:* Amish girls with their hair "let down" enjoy a fun time in the front yard of this house near Bird-In-Hand, Pennsylvania. *Below:* "Girl talk" takes place at this youth gathering at Jamesport, Missouri.

RECREATION

Amish boys and girls enjoy a spirited game of baseball such as seen here at the Twin Creek School near Becks Mills, Ohio. Girls are seated on the benches on the near side with the boys on the far side. *Above:* Volleyball is a favorite of youth in these scenes from *(Left)* Nickle Mines and Smoketown, Lancaster County, Pennsylvania.

Family outings by young couples give the adults time to catch-up on news of their families and give the children the opportunity to play. *Top, left*: At Honeyville, Indiana. *Lower, right*: Bonneyville Mill Park near Bristol, Indiana. *Top, right*: A buggy loaded with picnic supplies and chairs heads to a local picnic area in Lancaster County.

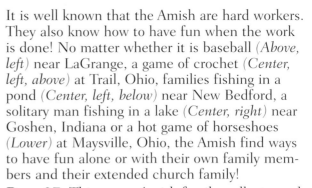

It is well known that the Amish are hard workers. They also know how to have fun when the work is done! No matter whether it is baseball *(Above, left)* near LaGrange, a game of crochet *(Center, left, above)* at Trail, Ohio, families fishing in a pond *(Center, left, below)* near New Bedford, a solitary man fishing in a lake *(Center, right)* near Goshen, Indiana or a hot game of horseshoes *(Lower)* at Maysville, Ohio, the Amish find ways to have fun alone or with their own family members and their extended church family!

Page 27. This young Amish family walks toward a bright sunrise on their way to Sunday church services near Winesburg, Ohio.

Above. Colorful yellow top buggies, found only in the Belleville area of the Big Valley, Pennsylvania, are parked around the yellow church wagon and large red barn at this farm. This scene was taken after church services had ended. Adults talk among themselves while the children play around the pond in the front yard. *Center:* A wagonload of benches is being delivered to the next host for church services at Mt. Hope, Ohio. *Lower, left:* An empty church wagon sits in front of the host family's house at Berlin, Ohio. *Lower, right:* Church benches are stored on the front porch of this house at Ethridge, Tennessee.

The host family's children unload benches from the church wagon, passing them through a first floor window into the main room, in preparation for the hosting of next Sunday's church services at New Bedford, Ohio.

SUNDAY CHURCH SERVICES

Sunday's church services begin around 8:30 a.m. Chores are completed early. Food, prepared the night before, is packed into baskets and loaded into the buggies or carried by hand. Families begin walking to church or riding their buggies early in the morning depending on the distance that they have to travel, either in their district or if they are going to another church district. Dressed in their Sunday clothes, immaculately washed and ironed, the Amish arrive at their host's home eager to participate in the worship service and the socialization afterwards. Men and boys line up on one side; women and girls on the other. They enter single file into the barn or house where services will be held. For the next three hours, they will sing songs from the *Ausbund* and listen to the sermon.

There are many ways for the Amish to get to their church services. In this scene at Nappanee, Indiana, the flat land makes it easy pedaling for the two wheel and three wheeled bicycles mixed in with the buggies.

Page 31. *Above, left and right:* Buggies and walkers arrive at the host farm for Sunday's church services at Charm, Ohio. *Center left:* The father pulls a small child along while the mother and an older girl walk to church at Nappanee, Indiana. *Center, right:* Three girls walk down a lane to the host farm at Bird-In-Hand, Pennsylvania. *Below:* Eight girls walk toward the host farm near New Bedford, Ohio, wearing traditional Holmes County church dresses.

Page 32. *Above, left:* A surrey arrives for church services near Berlin, Ohio. *Center:* Women and girls enter the barn before the start of church services near Maysville, Ohio. They will sit on the benches on the right side and the men and boys will sit on the left side. *Above, right:* The District Bishop, Deacon and Ministers walk out of the barn for a brief meeting before services are to begin. *Below, left:* Men's hats rest on tables on the front porch of this house hosting church services at Gap, Pennsylvania. *Below, right:* Boys sit and stand around talking before church services near Bartville, Pennsylvania.

Church services are held in these large Lancaster County barns at *(Above)* Intercourse and *(Below)* at Bird-In-Hand. The children play and their parents visit after church until mid afternoon, when they hitch up the buggy to return home.

WEDDINGS

Following a period of courtship, Amish couples are "published" (plans to get married are announced to the church district) during a church service from one to two weeks before their wedding day. Weddings are usually held in the fall once the busy harvest season has been completed. The wedding ceremony takes place on a Tuesday or a Thursday at the home of the bride. In keeping with their lifestyle, there are no rings, flowers or public display of affection. The bride and groom provide a small gift souvenir for the two hundred plus guests who attend the wedding. The ceremony usually starts at 8:30 a.m. and will last up to four hours. After the ceremony, the Amish wedding feast will begin and last until late evening. This is an elaborate "feast" with servers and numerous courses con-

Above: Three girls carry gifts as they walk to a nearby farm to attend a wedding ceremony at Becks Mills, Ohio. *Center*: The wedding corner is set up the day before the wedding as seen here at Mt. Hope, Ohio. The bride and groom and members of their wedding party are seated in this corner. *Below*: Guests arrive at the Mt. Hope, Ohio, home of the bride on the morning of the wedding.

34

sisting of roast beef, chicken, ham, stuffing, mashed potatoes, gravy, relishes, fruits and sweets, cookies, cakes and pies. Some weddings have so many guests that there are several seatings to accommodate them all.

Amish weddings unite the couple for life. Many marriages last sixty or seventy years; a few reach seventy-five years or more years in length. Couples typically have many grandchildren and great grandchildren.

ELDERS

Older Amish couples move into the *dawdy haus* after the young folk take over the farming. They will continue to help as long as they are able. This is where the retired couple will live and be taken care of in their old age.

Above: The smaller house to the right of the main house is the new dawdy haus.
Left: An elderly couple takes a slow walk down a long lane to their home near Charm, Ohio. Center and *Lower, right:* Older couples have time to visit their children and neighbors on their bicycle (*LaGrange, Indiana*) or run errands in town (*Belleville, Pennsylvania*).

FUNERALS

The Amish treat death as a natural part of life. A funeral is usually held three days after death. The body, placed in a plain wooden coffin without adornment, may be embalmed by a local funeral parlor and taken to the home of the deceased for viewing. On the day of the funeral, the coffin is placed on the back of a hack which, leading a long procession of buggies, carries the body to the cemetery. After a short graveside service, the coffin is lowered into the grave. There are no flowers and only a small tombstone is placed on the gravesite.

Above: A covered hack leads a funeral procession at Charm, Ohio, in an early morning funeral service. *Center, left:* Several hundred friends and relatives of the deceased attend this service near Middlefield, Ohio. *Center, right, above:* The funeral procession arrives at the cemetery near New Bedford, Ohio. *Center, right, below:* Simple tombstones mark graves at this Amish cemetery near Bird-In-Hand, Pennsylvania. *Below:* A long line of buggies crowds the shoulder of the roadway near Topeka, Indiana, at the gravesite.

HOUSES

The Amish live in comfortable houses, well insulated to provide warm protection from cold winters and open to keep cool in the hot summers. Their houses usually have four or more bedrooms which children share. Kitchens are large with space to fit a big table so that all family members can eat at one sitting.

Right: This Amish farm near Shipshewana, Indiana, consists of the main house, a barn and a number of sheds which house buggies and farm machinery. The kitchen garden provides both food and color. *Below:* The living room of this house looks much like that of any Englisher house. *Center, right:* The kitchen in this house near Charm, Ohio, has a natural gas burning cook stove, fed from a gas well found on the property, and hot and cold running water at the sink. *Below, right:* Many Amish purchase washing machines with the hand-cranked rollers and connect a gasoline engine to a belt to power the agitator like this one at Rexford, Montana.

Several features distinguish Amish farms: the windmill is the most noticeable and the kitchen garden is the most colorful. The windmill provides water for the family, its garden and livestock. The kitchen garden provides fresh vegetables and brightens the yard. Amish women use flower bouquets to add color to the kitchen and living rooms.

Above: Colorful flowers brighten this kitchen garden at Maysville, Ohio. The windmill is found on nearly every Amish owned farm. *Below:* A young boy plays while a woman works in this kitchen garden at Shipshewana, Indiana.

Monday is usually washday for the women. When the weather is cooperative, freshly washed clothing, both white and colors, adorn clotheslines all across America's Amish Country. Clotheslines shown here are from *(Above, left)* Nickle Mines, Pennsylvania, *(Above)* windblown Bloomfield, Iowa, *(Center, left)* calm Charlotte Hall, Maryland, *(Center, right)* cold and steamy Trail, Ohio, and *(Below)* colorful Walnut Creek, Ohio.

Above: This retired man still maintains a garden near Middlebury, Indiana. *Center:* This family kitchen garden near Topeka, Indiana, provides vegetables for immediate use as well as for canning. *Below, left:* These girls make quick work of shelling peas for their dinner table near New Wilmington, Pennsylvania. *Below, right:* A woman works in her kitchen garden near Topeka, Indiana.

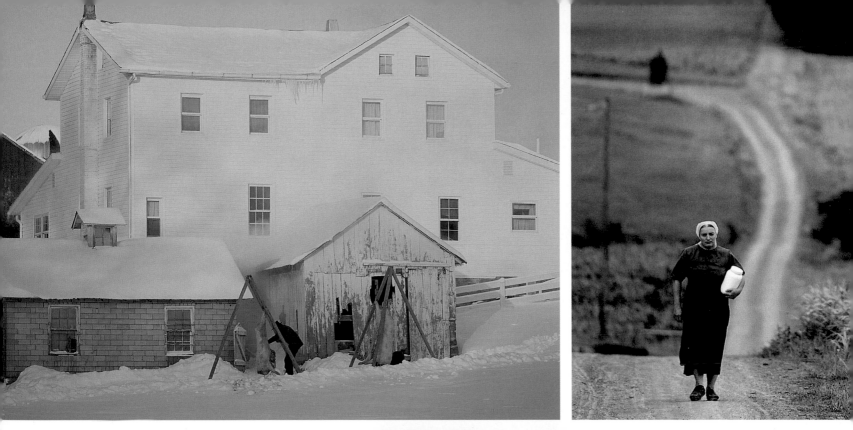

Above, left: This farmer butchers hogs at Farmerstown, Ohio. Some of the meat will be cured or kept frozen and the rest will be canned for future use. *Above, right:* Families that do not have cows will get fresh milk from a neighboring farm. *Center, Left:* A family picks feathers from chickens to prepare them for cooking or canning near Kenton, Ohio. *Center, right:* This hunter will have the large deer butchered at a local butcher shop. *Lower, left:* Some animals are sold for cash at the local livestock auction in Kidron, Ohio, rather than be butchered on the farm. *Lower, right:* An Amish family cuts ice on their pond to be used to keep food cold over the summer months.

41

Left: A young boy sets up the family produce stand in front of his house at De Peyster, New York, just after sunrise. He has placed tomatoes, yellow squash and white and red potatoes on the table. *Center:* With the mountains surrounding Big Valley as a spectacular backdrop, these girls lay out fresh corn for sale near Belleville. *Lower, left:* Women pick strawberries in the fields near Mesapotamia, Ohio. *Lower, right:* A woman sells strawberries from the back of a hack at Berlin, Ohio.

SELF RELIANCE

One of the enduring features of the Amish lifestyle is their ability to achieve self-reliance within their individual lives as well as within their community. They are able to raise crops to provide for their own needs yet have surplus to sell for

cash to purchase goods that they cannot readily produce. From stands at the end of the lane to organized farmer's markets, the Amish sell fresh produce and some baked and canned goods to nearby neighbors and the ever-increasing numbers of tourists.

Right: Fruit on sale at the market in Topeka, Indiana. *Center, left:* A young boy tosses cantaloupes to his brother as he unloads the wagon at the Mt. Hope Produce Auction near Mt. Hope, Ohio. *Center, right:* A Big Valley farmer and his daughter sell tomatoes at the Belleville, Pennsylvania, sales barn. He wears the traditional single suspender found only in the Big Valley. *Below:* A boy sells produce near Belleville while his Belgian horses wait patiently.

43

Local general stores (*Above*) at Mesapotamia, Ohio, and (*Below*) at Honeyville, Indiana, offer items that the Amish are unable to grow or make. *Inset:* They may also stop for a snack, pop or ice cream like this young girl at Belleville. *Center, right:* The telephone is increasingly being used to contact relatives in other states, order supplies and goods for the farm and to make Doctor's appointments. This "community" phone, complete with its own telephone directory written on the wall, is located near Nickel Mines, Pennsylvania.

As the Amish population has increased dramatically in the past forty years, so have the shortages of available land in the "traditional" Amish states of Pennsylvania, Ohio and Indiana. Many have adapted by changing from farming to selling goods, working in motor coach factories, repairing lawn mowers and small engines, building log houses, barns and making furniture. *Above, left:* This Amish man serves on the volunteer fire department at Gordonville, Pennsylvania, in keeping with the concept of service to his neighbors. *Above, right:* Meeting demand for repair of gasoline engines that power farm equipment, some Amish men have opened up repair shops for small engines and lawn mowers. *Center, right:* The Amish participate in estate and equipment auctions, such as this one near Topeka, Indiana, as a source for equipment used on their farms. *Center, left:* The Amish at Rexford, Montana, at the Canadian border, use teams of horses to haul timber down from the mountainsides. The harvested trees are used to build log houses and cabins, which are sold throughout the US. *Below, left:* Small lumber mills like this one near Winesburg, Ohio, also provide employment.

45

Above: Men arrive by the buggy loads to join in the barn raising already in progress at this farm near Maysville, Ohio. Over the next six pages, three barn raisings at Milroy, Pennsylvania and Maysville and Holmesville, Ohio, are featured. *Center, left:* The first main wall timbers are raised before daybreak at this Nebraska Amish farm at Milroy. When the sun does rise, (*Center, right, above*) near Milroy, and (*Below*) Maysville men are already hard at work completing the raising of the main wall timbers. *Center, right, below:* Workers cut large beams to fit at this barn raising near Mt. Hope, Ohio.

BARN RAISINGS

Another enduring feature of the Amish lifestyle, and perhaps the one for which they are best known, is their community involvement in a barn raising. Their ability to "raise" a barn in one day is well known throughout the world. It requires teamwork and cooperation from hundreds of neighbors, often involving local *Englishers*. Men, women and children come together for this involved task: men do the actual construction, with some help from the boys; women and girls do the cooking to feed everyone involved in the barn raising. A master barn builder coordinates the ordering and delivery of all materials. He and his crew, hired by the farmer whose barn is to be raised, oversee the volunteer workers.

Center: Men carry a large part of a wall to its place near Holmesville.
Below: The first walls go up near Holmesville in early morning.

47

At Maysville, construction is well underway by late morning with much of the main framing of the walls completed and some rafters installed. Teams work to complete their specific assignments as shown in the insets.

Left: Two Nebraska Amish use a table saw powered by a gasoline engine to cut trim pieces near Milroy. *Center:* An *Englisher (Left)* and an Amish man use a hand saw to cut a beam near Milroy. *Right:* These men are likely to have the experiences of many barn raisings to help guide them as they cut siding for the walls near Apple Creek, Ohio.

Left: Grandpas nail together a door near Apple Creek, Ohio, while a young boy watches to see how they are doing it. *Center* and *Right:* Near Holmesville, women watch as the first of the walls is raised into place.

The roof nears completion as walls are finished on the Holmesville barn. Young boys and *Englishers* watch the workers. *Insets:* Pencils and a nail sack and many hats are put aside when it is time for lunch. *Below:* Women serve lunch to men seated at long tables at Maysville.

Pages 51. Two girls prepare water for the workers to wash up before they eat.

Page 52. *Above:* Workers put the finishing touches to the roof near Holmesville, as most of the workers have gone home. *Center:* Nebraska Amish women watch as the roof and walls are completed near Milroy. *Below:* There are nine teams with discs working in this field near Walnut Creek, Ohio. When a farmer is ill or cannot work, neighbors will come to his aid and work his fields until he is again able to do so.

The threshing ring, once common among *Englisher's,* is another enduring example of how the Amish work together to harvest their crops. The ring (or circle) consists of men and boys from neighboring farms that work together to complete the harvesting of crops such as oats and corn. *Above:* A steam tractor is used to power a threshing machine near Charm, Ohio, as ring members from nearby farms bring wagonloads of oat shocks here to be threshed. During the summer and fall harvest seasons, the rings are busy as they move from farm to farm to help each other harvest their crops.

Above and *Right:* A steam tractor kept mostly as a hobby is used for powering this threshing machine at Becks Mills, Ohio. Two men feed sheaves of oats into the thresher from their wagon. *Below:* The operator stokes the fire in the firebox, keeping enough steam pressure to power the thresher.

Page 55. *Below:* A father loads oat sheaves to be threshed onto the farm wagon while his young son drives the team of Belgians.

FIELD WORK AND FARM EQUIPMENT

Field work is one of the more visible aspects of the Amish lifestyle. Teams of large draft horses, from two to eight either abreast or in tandem, pull various pieces of farm equipment to work the land from early spring until late fall. Amish farmers use many different farm implements to work their fields, plant and harvest crops and put up hay.

From ground breaking plows to hay bailing equipment, the teams, with their accompanying man or boy, walking or riding, create an impressive sight as they work their way across a field as shown on the following pages. While men and older boys do much of the work in the fields, girls and women also pitch in when needed.

Page 56. A team of Belgians pulls a grader to clear a heavy snowfall from the lane of this farmhouse near Mt. Hope, Ohio.

Above: A team pulls a "walking" plow through this large, snow-dusted field as spring plowing gets underway near Winesburg, Ohio. *Below:* An early snow catches these farmers putting corn shocks on a large wagon pulled by Belgians near Mt. Eaton, Ohio.

57

Page 58. A team of Belgians pulls a corn planter during spring planting in this field at Farmerstown, Ohio. A disc harrow sits near a hack used by the farmer to bring seed corn to be planted. *Inset:* A three-horse team pulls a riding plow at Honeyville in LaGrange County, Indiana.

Above, left: A women uses a team of Belgians and hay mower to cut weeds near LaGrange, Indiana. *Above, right:* A boy clears weeds with this cultivator at Kalona, Iowa.

Center, left: An Iowa farmer uses a hay rake while a hay lift, used to pile loose hay onto a wagon, sits nearby.

Center, right: Near Sugarcreek, Ohio, a team of four Belgians pulls a grain binder. *Below:* A hay bailer and hay wagon are used to clear this field near Barrs Mills, Ohio.

Page 60. Fall harvest in fields surrounded by colorful trees creates beautiful scenes from Holmes County, Ohio. *Above:* White Percherons pull a corn binder in this cornfield near Winesburg. *Below:* Belgians wait patiently with a large wagon as farmers harvest corn in this field near Becks Mills.

Right: Near Honeyville, Indiana, four Belgians pull a corn picker. *Below:* Farmers unload a wagon of corn stalk sheaves at Charm. The steam tractor powers a grinder-blower to create silage for storage in the silo.

Buggies used by the Amish come in all sizes and shapes and are designed for general or special purpose use.

Above: This is the driver's view from a buggy at Becks Mills, Ohio. *Center:* Milk hacks line up at Alpine Alpa Cheese at Wilmot, Ohio. *Below:* Family buggies, hacks and a green box wagon are lined up at the hitching post at the sale barn in Mt. Hope, Ohio.

Page 63. *Above, left:* A Yoder, Kansas, buggy is decorated with reflector tape. *Above, center:* This youth's buggy at Yoder has fancy decorations. *Above, right:* In northern Indiana, a number of buggies tow trailers as seen here at Topeka. *Center:* Large family buggies are common in LaGrange County, Indiana.

Not all buggies are black as illustrated on these pages. Some groups of Amish have chosen different colors so that they can be readily distinguished from the other groups. *Above, left:* A brown top buggy pulls a trailer at New Wilmington, Pennsylvania. *Above, right:* This youth's buggy has the distinguishing rounded side and bottom of the settlement at Dover, Delaware. *Below:* Hacks at the auction at Topeka, Indiana, are seen in reflections in a water puddle.

Page 65. *Above:* Gray top buggies are found in Lancaster County, Pennsylvania. *Center, left:* Yellow top buggies are used at Belleville, Pennsylvania.

Center, right: Garfield is right at home on this youth's buggy near Spring Garden, Pennsylvania. *Lower:* White top buggies are used by the Nebraska Amish at Belleville, Pennsylvania.

Page 66. *Above, left:* Buggies at Arcola, Illinois, are parked under cover to protect the horses from the hot sun. *Above, right:* An Amish family uses a small, air filled, rubber tire wagon at Nappanee, Indiana. *Right:* The use of oxen is very rare but a few are kept, mostly as a hobby, near Farmerstown, Ohio. *Center:* Buggies of all kinds are tied up at a school at Honeyville, Indiana. *Lower, left and right:* Despite warning signs, such as this sign in Holmes County, Ohio, urging car drivers to use caution, accidents between cars and buggies sometimes happen. Farm accidents happen as well, like this hay wagon that was upset near Millersburg, Indiana. *Right:* This used buggy at Becks Mills, Ohio, is available today for only $850.00.

Above: A wagon is used to haul coal near Maysville, Ohio, while buggies (*Center, right*) wait in line for road construction to be completed near Farmerstown, Ohio. *Below:* A black buggy heads into the bright orange glow of an Ohio sunset near Walnut Creek.

Page 68. *Above, left:* A black-smith at Sugar Creek replaces the shoe on a horse. *Above, right:* Harness and tack line the wall of this barn at Charm, Ohio. *Center and Below:* Many Amish use bicycles to travel around the flat land of northern Indiana.

Above: Two men sit in a buggy at Walnut Creek, Ohio, looking at an Ohio Amish Directory which lists all Holmes County and vicinity Amish church members and their families. *Below:* A horse patiently waits for its owner to return from this snow covered farm at Bunker Hill, Ohio, so that they can continue their rounds of delivering Christmas gifts. Amish people exchange gifts and celebrate Christmas on December 25th and Old Christmas (Epiphany) on January 6th, but they do not decorate as *Englishers* do.

69

OHIO

A team of five Percherons pulls a riding plow on this farm with a large barn and many buildings used to store equipment, buggies and hay at Bunker Hill.

The Amish settlements in Ohio are well established with the largest number in Holmes County. The beautiful rolling hills, dotted with large farms, are colorful during all seasons. A farmer uses a spring tooth harrow near Kidron as the sun sets low in the west.

Six Belgians pull a riding plow while working this field blanketed in early morning ground fog near Mt. Eaton.

Above: Green grass and green hills form a picturesque setting near Charm as this team of five Belgians pull a disc to prepare the field for planting. *Below, right:* A farmer uses a riding plow to turn under a field of rye near Bunker Hill, disturbing a milk cow that had been grazing on the grass.

Above: Two young boys drive a wagon home near Maysville in Wayne County. *Below:* Fog nearly hides blooming daffodils as a buggy passes by on a spring morning going towards Farmerstown in Holmes County.

Page 74. Lush green grass covers the hills as trees bud out above this boy preparing soil for planting with a disc near Calais in Noble County. His father mends a fence in the field behind him.

Page 75. Green pastures surround this winding road, framed by a blooming apple tree, near Becks Mills in Holmes County.

Page 76. *Above:* A team of Belgians pulls a wagon and reluctant heifers to spring pasture near Middlefield in Geauga County. *Center, left:* A buggy passes through a backlit grove of trees near New Bedford in Holmes County. *Center, right:* Children jump on a trampoline at Farmerstown. *Below:* A boy guides a team of Belgians as they pull a cultivator near Fredericksburg in Holmes County.

Men load loose hay on a wagon driven by a young boy near Mt. Hope in Holmes County. *Inset:* Two teams work in a hay field near Becks Mills with a hay mower *(right)* and a hay rake *(left)*.

Pages 78-79. A farmer works to bind oats in this large field as a buggy passes by going towards Charm.

Pages 80-81. White farmhouses and barns sit amidst a sea of green pastures, cornfields and oat shocks in this spectacular scene at Farmerstown.

Page 82. A team of Belgians pulls a grain binder down a hill near New Bedford.

A wagon in a field of shocked corn is silhouetted against fog in early morning light near New Bedford. *Inset:* Near Winesburg, men load loose hay onto a wagon just before sunset on a hot summer evening.

Fall foliage paints the trees in beautiful bright colors in these scenes from Holmes County. *Above, left:* A buggy is silhouetted against a field of shocked corn laced with morning fog at sunrise near New Bedford. *Above, right:* A boy doing his chores loads firewood into a box wagon near Becks Mills. *Below:* Buggies heading for church pass on a road through a brightly colored tunnel of fall foliage near Bunker Hill.

A large group of school children walk home from their nearby schoolhouse close to New Bedford. *Inset:* Children arrive at their schoolhouse covered with smoke from a hot fire in the wood heater near Mt. Eaton.

Fall foliage and the harvest season herald the end of warm weather and the beginning of cold winter months just ahead. A buggy near Trail, Ohio passes a field of shocked corn and bright orange colored leaves. *Below:* A team of three white horses pulls a forecart down the road, followed closely by a hack, toward this farm just outside of Winesburg in Holmes County.

The chill of winter is felt in these early snow and ice scenes. *Above:* A buggy negotiates an ice-covered road besides a fence and trees sparkling in the early morning sun near Berlin. *Center:* A sunset paints the sky near Fredericksburg in Wayne County. *Below:* A light coat of snow covers these farm buildings and field at sunrise near Mt. Hope.

A heavy snowfall has covered this road and surrounding trees, painting a beautiful scene at Fredericksburg. *Inset:* Buggies pass a house and field of shocked corn at Mt. Eaton.

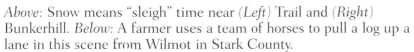
Above: Snow means "sleigh" time near *(Left)* Trail and *(Right)* Bunkerhill. *Below:* A farmer uses a team of horses to pull a log up a lane in this scene from Wilmot in Stark County.

PENNSYLVANIA

Page 90. Some of the Amish families that first arrived in Pennsylvania in the 1720s settled in the area around Lancaster. The gentle rolling hills of Lancaster are covered with farms in the best-known Amish settlement. *Above:* A gray top buggy, the color utilized by the Amish of Lancaster County, heads down a long road near Spring Garden. *Below:* A team of mules pulls a compactor in a field near Intercourse. Mules and horses are used for fieldwork in Lancaster County.

Above: A six-mule team pulls a disc with a large white farmhouse and barn in the background near Intercourse. *Below:* Farms line the road as far as the eye can see at Bird-In-Hand.

Big Valley, in Mifflin County, is an exceptionally beautiful valley that runs from Reedsville in the northeastern end to Mill Creek on the southwestern end. It includes a rich mix of Amish culture and lifestyles, buggies and farms. The Valley includes the towns of Allensville, Barrville, Belleville, Menno, Milroy and Reedsville. Traditional black buggies are used by Reno Amish; the Byler Amish use buggies with yellow tops and the Nebraska Amish use white tops. Men in the Valley use only one-strap suspenders with the exception of the Nebraska Amish who do not use any suspenders. The field scene shows a farmer using a grain binder near Belleville to harvest his crop of oats.

Above: Lancaster County is still graced by numerous covered bridges. A buggy is about to enter the Jackson Mills Covered Bridge near Bartville. *Center:* A buggy passes by a field of flowers coming from Intercourse. *Below:* A brown top buggy is used only at New Wilmington in Lawrence County.

Page 95. An open buggy slowly climbs a hill overlooking several large farms at Bartville. The long, flat building directly above the buggy is a commercial chicken house.

Above: Young boys guide a team of large Belgians pulling a forecart and wagon at Belleville. *Center, left:* Tobacco dries in this barn at Strasburg. While only a few Amish are known to use tobacco and tobacco products, many Amish farmers in Lancaster County grow it as a cash crop. *Center, right:* A tractor pulls a threshing machine down the road near Belleville. *Lower:* A family harvests tobacco near Intercourse.

Page 97. *Above:* Men work near Milroy to pile loose hay on their horse drawn wagon. *Below:* A grain binder is used to harvest oats on this large farm with huge silos near Belleville.

Above, left and right: White top buggies pass beautiful farms near Reedsville. *Lower, left:* A young boy and girl take a shortcut across a field at Belleville. *Lower, right:* A four-horse team pulls a hay rake after crossing through the Logan Mill Covered Bridge near Logantown in Clinton County.

Above: Boys use a hack to tow a boat for an afternoon of fishing near New Wilmington. *Below:* A little boy looks back as his father guides their hack along a dirt and gravel road near Reedsville.

Above and Center: The Nebraska Amish use kerosene lanterns on each side of their buggies as shown here near Reedsville. *Below:* Two Belgians pull a wagonload of cornstalks near New Wilmington.

Page 101. A family buggy goes down a dirt lane toward a large farmhouse with huge red barns near Summit Mills in Somerset County.

Pages 102-103. Big Valley is quite beautiful in all seasons. This winter scene shows dozens of farms and fields with corn shocks protruding up from the snow.

Page 102. *Left:* Yellow top buggies pass on an ice-covered lane where church is being held near Belleville. *Right:* Children take advantage of the snow to do some sledding near Belleville.

Page 103. *Left:* Milk cans sit on a roadside stand for pickup just outside of Milroy. Church service is being held at this Nebraska Amish farmhouse. *Right:* A two-horse team pulls a wagon equipped with runners near Belleville.

INDIANA

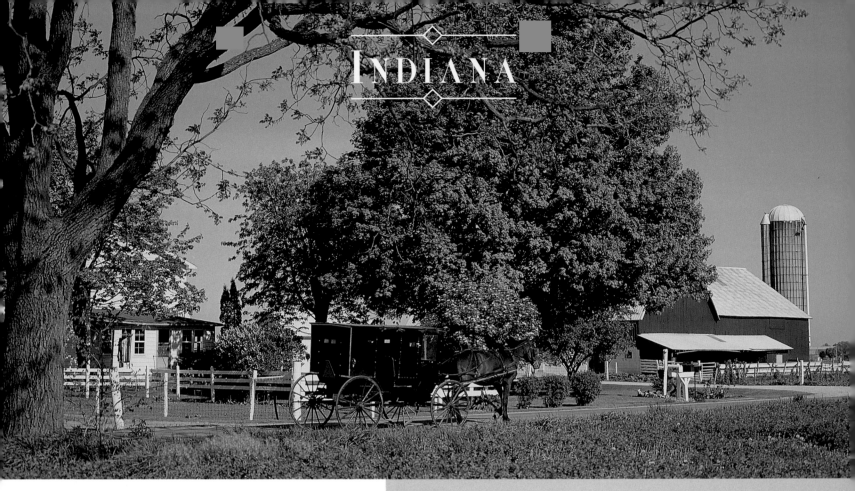

Indiana is home to the third largest population of Amish settlements. Most of the Amish are located in northern Indiana in the counties of Elkhart, LaGrange, Kosciusko and Marshall. *Above:* The green of summer covers the flat land of northern Indiana as a typically larger family buggy goes towards LaGrange in LaGrange County. *Below:* An open buggy near Berne in Adams County heads for church on an early Sunday morning. *Inset:* A gray top buggy, recently relocated from Lancaster County, Pennsylvania, passes blooming dogwood going towards Rockville in Parke County.

A six-horse team of Belgians pulls a disc during spring plowing near Nappanee in Elkhart County. *Inset:* An open buggy bound for church near Berne has just crossed into Ohio as children look out of the back.

Pages 106-107. Fog nearly blankets this farmhouse at Honeyville in LaGrange County as a buggy passes by a field of soybeans.

Page 106. *Inset:* A buggy is silhouetted near Shipshewana, known locally as Shipshe, just after sunrise.

Inset, left: A buggy emerges from a shroud of fog on this tree lined road near LaGrange in LaGrange County. *Inset, below:* Just before sunset near LaGrange, a farmer and his team of four Belgian draft horses finish up their field work with a grain binder.

Above: A team of Belgians pulls this grain binder near Topeka in LaGrange County. *Below:* A couple walk to church while a buggy passes on the road to Goshen in Elkhart County.

Page 109. *Above:* At Emma, in LaGrange County, a couple takes a boat out of the water after a day of fishing. *Below:* A young girl looks out at a bright row of sunflowers near Nappanee in Elkhart County.

Page 110. Near Shipshe, a wagonload of loose hay is being pulled to the barn by a team of Belgians.

Above, left: A buggy passes a row of flowers near Shipshe. *Above, right:* A lone horse and buggy are tied up at the hitching post of the Honeyville General Store, a well-stocked store with goods for the nearby Amish and a local tourist attraction. *Center:* A buggy heads out the lane on its way into Topeka to run an errand. *Below:* A strong team of Belgians pulls a double hitch of hay wagons near LaGrange.

A large, open family buggy passes by a brightly colored garden near Topeka.

Page 114. *Above, left:* A team of Haflingers, pulls away from a feed mill near LaGrange to make a delivery with this bulk feed wagon. *Above, right:* Two farmers stop to chat on this road near Topeka. *Below:* Reflection of a passing buggy in this pond near Topeka makes a lovely scene.

Above: A buggy passes a schoolhouse near Nappanee. *Below, left:* A team of Belgians, pulling a forecart, is on its way to work in a field near Topeka. *Below, right:* This lovely maple tree creates a beautiful scene near Topeka.

Fall colors and falling leaves from this tree near
Topeka means that winter cannot be far away.

Above: Near Shipshe, a sleigh is used to take advantage of the deep snow. Regular buggies were used by children to get to the school in the background. *Below:* Boys play hockey and girls skate on this pond during school recess near LaGrange.

117

NORTHERN STATES

◆ Michigan ◆ New York ◆ Maine ◆

A brilliantly colored tree stands in sharp contrast to the black buggy near Centerville, Michigan.

Above: A woman heads for Stanwood, Michigan, on an errand. *Center, left:* A woman grinds sorghum to make molasses near California, Michigan. *Center, right:* A girl washes a buggy at Conewango, New York. *Center, below:* A group of boys walks home from school through a snow-covered field near Conewango. *Below, left:* An elderly couple uses an open hack to run an errand near Conewango. *Below, right:* Maple syrup buckets hang from trees as a woman hangs her wash on the clothesline just outside of Conewango. The rich sap collected from the trees will be used to make flavorful maple syrup.

Page 120. *Inset, above:* Two boys sell corn beside the highway at Conewango. *Inset, below:* A family rides in their buggy past a field of oat shocks.

Near Conewango, New York, the Conewango Valley is a beautiful area as these scenes show. A farmer delivers milk to a local pickup point as the sun rises. *Inset:* Quilts and clothes hang out to dry on a clothesline stretching from the house to the barn.

The Amish settlements in Ontario are located in the rich farmland at Aylmer and around Millbank and Milverton. This field scene with two girls picking up oat sheaves is at Millbank. *Inset, right:* A farmer uses a grain binder to harvest his field at Desbro. **Pages 122-123.** *Insets, below, left and right:* Open buggies, such as these at Milverton, are used throughout Ontario. **Page 123.** *Inset, above:* A father and young son work to harvest loose hay at Desbro.

SOUTHERN STATES

◆ Delaware ◆ Maryland ◆ Virginia ◆ West Virginia ◆
◆ North Carolina ◆ Florida ◆ Tennessee ◆ Kentucky ◆

A field of sunflowers, foreground, and tobacco surrounds this farmhouse near Charlotte Hall, Maryland. The gray top buggy indicates that this settlement was started by Amish from Lancaster County, Pennsylvania. *Inset, right:* Sunday church services are held a meetinghouse near Union Grove, North Carolina.

Page 125. *Inset, above:* A buggy passes a large white barn and farmhouses at Dover, Delaware. *Inset, below:* Three children walk along a road at Union Grove, North Carolina, pulling a homemade wagon.

An Amish father takes his children to school, accompanied by the family dogs, in Burkes Garden, Virginia, prior to heading off to do fieldwork. *Inset:* A light snow dusts farm equipment waiting for use in the spring in Burkes Garden.

Page 127. *Inset, above, left:* A mother and her daughters work in the kitchen garden in front of this house at Dover, Delaware. *Inset, above, right:* A husband rides this three-wheel bicycle, while his wife walks alongside, past orange trees at Pinecraft Park in Sarasota, Florida. *Inset, below, left:* A buggy passes a dogwood tree in full bloom near Park City, Kentucky. *Inset, above, right:* Three men play a game of basketball at Pinecraft Park.

Page 128. A buggy returning from Horse Cave, Kentucky, passes through an archway of trees.

Above: At Ethridge, Tennessee, a buggy goes by a large farm on a dirt road. *Center, left:* A buggy at Marion, Kentucky, follows a gravel covered road. *Center, right, above:* Children work in a garden at Ethridge. *Center, right, below:* A little boy rides a work-horse while his father rides on a sled. *Below:* A young couple on a hack near Marion splash across a ford on a creek on roads built by the Amish after purchasing a 5000 acre tract of land and dividing it into over a dozen farms.

WESTERN STATES

◆ Illinois ◆ Wisconsin ◆ Iowa ◆ Missouri ◆ Texas ◆ Oklahoma ◆
◆ Kansas ◆ Minnesota ◆ Montana ◆ Washington ◆

The flat farmland around Arcola and Arthur, Illinois, produces bountiful crops of corn, oats and hay. This buggy, at Arthur, goes past a field with oat shocks.

Page 130. *Inset:* A farmer uses a grain binder to harvest this field of oats near Kalona, Iowa.

Inset, left: Buggies line up at the hitching post at Yoder, Kansas. *Inset, right, above:* The Amish at Chouteau, Oklahoma, use tractors for fieldwork due to the extreme heat conditions. *Inset, below:* A little girl gets a ride in a wagon pulled by her mother near Bloomfield, Iowa.

An hour in the life of the Amish at Jamesport, Missouri, illustrates the types of conveyances that a settlement may use. *Above, left:* A man uses a two-wheel cart to move a barrel. *Above, right:* A mother and children use a road cart to run an errand. *Center:* A young boy leads a team of Belgians towards a large farm in the distance. *Below, left:* Another young boy drives a team of Belgians pulling a cultivator behind. *Below, right:* Two girls and a boy ride in the back of an *Englisher* neighbor's pickup truck.

Above: An open buggy comes up the lane from this farm near Seymour, Missouri, as the man and woman go to church. *Center:* A father holds his infant daughter as the mother carries a basket filled with food to be eaten after church services at Diggins, Missouri. *Below:* A buggy goes towards a farm with a large red barn near Cashton, Wisconsin.

A buggy goes down the lane toward this farm
under a rainbow at Harmony, Minnesota.